Real Life Psychic Detectives

True Crime Stories of Clairvoyants Solving Murder Cases

Jack Smith

Copyrights

All rights reserved. © Jack Smith (2017) and Maplewood Publishing (2017). No part of this publication or the information in it may be quoted from or reproduced in any form by means such as printing, scanning, photocopying, or otherwise without prior written permission of the copyright holder.

Disclaimer and Terms of Use

Effort has been made to ensure that the information in this book is accurate and complete. However, the author and the publisher do not warrant the accuracy of the information, text, and graphics contained within the book due to the rapidly changing nature of science, research, known and unknown facts, and internet. The author and the publisher do not hold any responsibility for errors, omissions, or contrary interpretation of the subject matter herein. This book is presented solely for motivational and informational purposes only.

Warning

Throughout the book there are some descriptions of murders and crime scenes that some people might find disturbing.

Note

Words in italic are quoted words from verbatim and have been reproduced as is, including any grammatical errors and misspells.

For Jack Smith author's page on Amazon, please click here

For Jack Smith Facebook page, please click here

ISBN: 978-1979839402

Printed in the United States

Avant-Propos

They call it extrasensory perception. But when worried families hire dogged paranormal private investigators to look into the disappearance of their loved ones, they just call it "getting results." It is usually when all other means have been exhausted that these desperate people find themselves laying bare their tragic circumstances to a clairvoyant—and their success rate is nothing to sneeze at! This book presents cases that would have gone unsolved if not for the intervention of a psychic detective. Get yourself acquainted with these 12 thought-provoking, incredible true stories of clairvoyant crime solving.

Contents

An Extrasensory Witness ... 1
Noreen Gets It Right ... 3
Flowers for Sale ... 9
Ashley Howley's Post Mortem Psychic Reading ... 15
Tragedy at a Picnic ... 19
Andre Daigle's Last Night Out ... 27
The Jewel Thief ... 35
The Psychic Gamble ... 41
The Party Gone Bad ... 47
The Baton Rouge Serial Killer ... 55
Running from Justice ... 61
What Happened to Patrick? ... 67
Daryl Cozart's Fickle Friends ... 71
Just a Case of Extrasensory Perception ... 81
Also by Jack Smith ... 83
Appendix A: Further Reading and Resources ... 85

An Extrasensory Witness

In most cases of murder there is no witness. Aside from crimes of passion, mass shootings, and other rare cases where the murderer does not care who sees him, these crimes are usually meticulously hidden from the public. Most killers strike their victims when they are all alone and no one else can see or assist them. It is for this reason that forensic science so often becomes the silent witness to a crime scene.

Since no one can tell investigators exactly what happened, they use DNA and other forensic evidence to lead them to the truth. But as good as DNA evidence is, it is not always available—and despite what you may have heard, it is sometimes unreliable. Notwithstanding its great success rate, DNA is not a silver bullet that nabs the bad guys every single time. There are many cases that remain unsolved with no clear evidence and no clear leads to follow.

It is usually for these cases that "psychic detectives" are called in to see what they can find out. These gifted individuals claim to have special abilities that can send their minds backwards and forwards in time in order to envision what took place. For an experienced clairvoyant, it's like a movie played in his mind, and he can fast forward, rewind, and pause until he gathers enough information to tell the story.

Although they were not physically present when the crime occurred, they become in a sense extrasensory witnesses after the fact. The stories presented in this book are true, and the uncanny manner in which these psychics solved crimes that had stumped the experts remains as a permanent testament to just how powerful an extrasensory witness can be.

Noreen Gets It Right

It was a sad scene to witness: an elderly couple shot execution-style in the head, their corpses splayed out in their own living room. Jake and Dora Cohn were a retired couple with no known enemies, living a simple life off of Jake's pension from a career as a milk man. What reason would anyone have to so brutally end their lives? This was the quandary that confronted seasoned investigator Lieutenant Ray Krolak when he began working on this case.

Though little more than a hunch (hardnosed investigator slang for mild ESP), Krolak's suspicions initially fell on the Cohns' grandson, James Mariani. This hunch was based mostly on the poor character of the suspect and his odd behavior shortly after his grandparents' demise. We are usually told it isn't polite to make snap judgments about other people—but when you are a seasoned investigator, the snap judgment is sometimes your biggest lead.

Mariani raised the detective's eyebrows by requesting a copy of the Cohns' will almost immediately after hearing about their untimely death. But just because Mariani was insensitive (and perhaps even morbidly greedy), that does not necessarily make him a murderer. There are plenty of spoiled grandchildren out there who are cold and callous enough to start sniffing around for an inheritance as soon as their relatives have passed on.

And in this case, it was soon discovered that Mariani had an airtight alibi. There was no way he could have been physically present on the night that the Cohns were killed. As this dead end stared him in the face, the no-nonsense Lieutenant Krolak began to consider something he had never thought he would: enlisting the aid of a psychic.

Noreen Renier wasn't just any psychic, however; she was a 30-year veteran psychic detective with multiple solved cases already under her belt. It wasn't a career path that Noreen had planned; it came as a spontaneous calling when she was a young girl and her nascent psychic abilities mysteriously manifested themselves. By the time she crossed paths with Krolak, her psychic mind had already been sharpened to a razor's edge.

When Krolak finally decided to give Noreen a call, she requested that he supply her with some of the victims' personal items. This seemed pretty bizarre to Krolak, but his desire to close the Cohn case urged him forward. He retrieved one of Jake's shoes and a pair of Dora's glasses from the evidence locker and sent them to Noreen.

When she received the items, Noreen laid her hands on them and focused. Then, like she was tuning into some invisible radio signal, she began to pick up information about the victims and how they met their demise.

The first thing she pictured was Doreen sitting in her home by the telephone. Suddenly, the front door burst open as a man kicked it in. As Noreen channeled Dora's experience, she got the feeling that this man was no stranger. It was someone that Dora and her husband knew fairly well. This man was someone who had done some kind of work in their home. He had even eaten in with them in their house on occasion.

This man was no stranger, and the couple undoubtedly knew his name, but as much as Noreen tried to focus on that name, it was not forthcoming. Instead of a full name, she just kept perceiving the initials "RS". In her vision, Noreen saw this mysterious "RS" aim his gun and kill Jake Cohn as his wife looked on in horror, before she too succumbed to the murderer's bullet.

Krolak was impressed by what he heard, but in order to vet this psychic detective he requested copies of her phone records. He wanted to make sure that Noreen wasn't getting her information from anywhere else. After checking out her phone calls, however, Krolak became entirely convinced that Noreen was the real deal. He then set out to see if he could find the murderer Noreen referred to as RS. It didn't take long for Krolak to find a likely candidate for his extrasensory suspect.

He came upon some of the couple's financial records and discovered that they had recently hired the services of a local carpenter by the name of Robert Skinner. Could the initials RS stand for Robert Skinner? It seemed like too much of a coincidence to ignore. Skinner had apparently been scheduled to tile the floors of the Cohn house. He was said to lay a pretty mean piece of ceramic tile, but Skinner wasn't just a handyman. He had a long criminal record as well.

He had some significant links to the underworld of Schenectady, New York, and in these more nefarious circles Skinner was often in cahoots with a fellow hood named Keith Snare—who was said to be quite experienced in the act of kicking down doors. As damning as these findings may seem, however, Krolak still had no concrete evidence against the two.

The case once again stalled, but then the police department received a phone call from an informant. This informant told them that he'd recently seen the two suspects at a party—and this party had been particularly memorable because Robert Skinner had accidentally discharged his gun. Realizing that this gun could be the same one that killed the Cohns, police got the homeowner's permission to dig up his carpet and search for the bullet.

But after ballistics testing, it was discovered that the bullet did not match. The gun Skinner fired at the party was not the same one used to kill the Cohns. Skinner was also found to have an airtight alibi, so once again there was no basis for an arrest warrant.

Krolak's doubts began to resurface. He started to wonder if this so-called psychic had done nothing more than risk his professional reputation by sending him on a wild goose chase. In order to allay his fears, Noreen agreed to meet him in person. For this meeting, Krolak brought a lineup of ten photos, including all the current suspects, just to see what kind of reaction he could get out of the psychic. Surprisingly, Noreen refused to look at the pictures. Instead, she asked Krolak to lay them all out face down on the table. She then waved her hand over the back of each one of the pictures, as if she were gathering the essence of each photograph with the mere sweep of her hand.

After going back and forth like this for a few minutes, Noreen took seven of the photos off of the table. Focusing on one of the three remaining pictures, she turned it over. It was none other than Robert Skinner, the one she had long known as RS, who was staring back at them. She then pointed to the picture next to his and flipped it over, indicating that the subject—Skinner's longtime door-kicking accomplice Keith Snare—was involved in the crime as well. Having saved the best for last, Noreen then flipped over the third picture to reveal the Cohns' own grandson—whom she now proclaimed to be the mastermind who had planned the whole crime.

But what about the rock-solid alibis that all three men had? According to Noreen, all of these alibis were fabrications prearranged by Mariani in order to cover their tracks. She insisted that Krolak go back and check the alibis of these two men.

Sure enough, after the investigative team took a closer look, these alibis proved to have more holes than Swiss cheese. First of all, Robert Skinner who had claimed that he was out on a date listening to a rock concert on the day in question, was found to have been doing no such thing. In fact, the woman he claimed to have been with had been nowhere near him. In other words, his alibi had been a complete lie.

This was enough to take all three men to trial, and after all of the arguments had been made they were found guilty for their respective roles in the crime and received sentences to match. Skinner received the longest term of 62 years, while his accomplice Keith Snare was given a 40-year sentence. Mariani also received 40 years for his role in masterminding the whole operation. Thanks to a relentless and uncannily accurate psychic detective, this case was solved.

Flowers for Sale

It was a truly tragic scene: a woman in the prime of her life cut down in broad daylight in the most brutal fashion. The only thing that surpassed the tragedy of Diana Goldston's death was the senselessness of it. It has been over 20 years now since she was gunned down in front of a Texas bar, and although her killers have been apprehended, the motive behind the crime remains a complete mystery.

The assailant produced a half-baked story that this frail florist had stolen hundreds of dollars out of his truck. But even if that story didn't seem completely ridiculous to begin with, it was immediately contradicted by eyewitnesses who saw this big, burly man and his girlfriend confront Diana Goldston and then force her into the cab of his truck. There was no argument over money, just a young woman being manhandled, shot and thrown into a truck.

It could be regarded as an amazing testament to human indifference that no one thought to intervene directly. One bystander did call 911, though, and police eventually made it onto the scene. Unfortunately, it was far too late for Diana, who had already been driven away bleeding profusely in the back of the strange couple's vehicle.

Even though this assault had been witnessed in broad daylight by several patrons of the local tavern, police quickly found that they had no leads whatsoever. No one had had the presence of mind to take down a license plate number, and none of them even knew Diana's name; they had simply referred to her as "Flower Girl." She was not identified until her mother called up the police department to report that she had not seen or heard from her daughter for a couple of days. She said that the last thing Diana had told her was that she was going down to a local bar to sell flowers, and the police quickly connected the dots.

As they began to build a profile of their victim, they found that she had no known enemies. The brutal act was seeming more and more like a case of random violence. Investigators were at a loss when someone recommended that they consult with an experienced psychic detective by the name of Carol Pate. Most of the standard variety detectives looking into Diana's disappearance were skeptical to say the least, but after exhausting virtually all other resources, even the most ardent skeptics among them were willing to give Carol a try.

Lead investigator Kenny Kirkland met Carol in person and after a brief interview brought her directly to the crime scene to see what she could pick up. Kirkland wasn't disappointed. Although she had been given next to no details about the case, Carol began to tune in to Diana's last moments. She soon had visions of Diana being confronted by the man and woman, being shot in the shoulder, and then being viciously shoved into a black pickup truck. None of these details had been released to the public, so Carol should have had no way of knowing them.

She zeroed in on the suspects and began to get a clearer picture of them. She described the man as being very large and decidedly unkempt, with an out-of-control temper. According to the psychic, after the shooting, this big, burly man feared that he had killed Diana. He panicked and threw her in the truck, planning to dispose of her body and conceal his crime. But Carol perceive that that Diana was still alive at that point.

Impressed by Carol's uncanny intuition about the background of the case, investigators pressed her to lead them from the crime scene to where Diana was taken. Getting in a car with a police detective, Carol directed him where to drive as she scanned the surrounding area with her clairvoyant perception. She later claimed that almost as soon as they left the parking lot, everything simply "fell into place" and she "knew exactly where to go."

As she led the police along, it was as if some sort of psychic GPS system was giving her turn-by-turn directions in her head! She took them to a wooded area on the edge of town, saying that she felt the distinct impression that Diana had been dropped off there but removed later on. Investigators were baffled as to why Diana's corpse would have been moved like that, but after releasing cadaver dogs and searching the area, they came to believe that Carol was correct.

They found plenty of signs that a dead or dying Diana had been in the area, including a bloody sheet that had the clear outline of a body on its surface, as if someone had been wrapped up in it like a shroud. This sad excuse for a burial shroud was delivered to a forensics lab and subjected to a battery of tests. Although it was absolutely certain that it was covered with human blood, the DNA had deteriorated to such an extent that no definitive match to Diana could be made.

As detectives found themselves back at square one, they turned to Carol Pate once again. They took her on a car ride to retrace the possible path of Diana's killers, and this time Carol led them to a nearby state park. They parked at the main gate and followed Carol the psychic detective as she walked into the park. As they continued on, Carol had clairvoyant visions of Diana being dragged through the woods.

Diana was still alive at this point, and although she had lost a lot of blood, she was struggling to stay conscious. The murderers first left her in the middle of the woods, out in the open, to bleed to death. However, when they noticed someone walking nearby, they panicked once again, picked her up, and took her to yet another location.

As they were following this lead, investigators scoured the area searching for tire marks or any other evidence that the perpetrators might have left behind. Sure enough, they found a muddy depression in the woods where a large vehicle such as a truck had apparently been stuck. Drag marks led from this location, seeming to verify what the psychic had told them; Diana had indeed been moved. The search for her final resting place then began anew.

Following indentations in the ground, investigators found another piece of the puzzle: a woman's yellow jacket. Diana had last been seen in a bright yellow jacket. Also of tragic significance, this particular yellow jacket's left shoulder was covered in blood, corresponding exactly to where Diana's gunshot wound was believed to have been. It didn't take a psychic premonition for the police to deduce that this article of clothing had belonged to Diana.

With Carol in tow, investigators tracked down one of the state park ranger and asked him if he had witnessed anything unusual in the past couple of days. The ranger remembered a truck that had been stuck in the mud—and he'd had the presence of mind to take down its license plate number. Investigators quickly seized upon this bit of information, ran the plate, and discovered that the truck was owned by a woman named Carrie Griffin.

Police dispatched to Ms. Griffin's house questioned her and discovered that although the plates were in her name, she did not drive the vehicle they were on. The truck was instead driven by her ex-husband, a local man named Jason Robert "J.R." Griffin. Investigators also learned that J.R. was currently living with a girlfriend named Janet Cox.

The police showed up at the couple's house and discovered J.R.'s pickup truck parked in the driveway. Despite protests from the couple, they searched the truck—and found a gun along with a large amount of blood splattered all throughout the vehicle. The gun itself was also covered in blood, both inside and out. With such damning evidence, the two suspects were immediately taken into police custody.

Although J.R. remained defiant, Janet Cox appeared ready to make a confession. According to her, she was the one who first approached Diana on that fateful day, walking up to her and asking, "Are you the flower girl?" When Diana replied that she was, Janet struck up a conversation about an upcoming wedding she was going to participate in and asked her if she "did weddings."

This was all apparently a ruse, however. As Janet continued to talk with Diana, she led her right to J.R.'s truck. As they approached, the burly man jumped out and pulled a gun on the frightened girl. J.R. and Janet then tried to force the young woman into the truck with them, shooting her in the struggle that ensued. Although the police never did find Diana's body, this confession, coupled with DNA evidence and the testimony of a certain psychic, was enough to put them away.

The jurors at their trial found both J.R. and Janet guilty of aggravated kidnapping, which in Texas carries a life sentence. If it wasn't for Carol's extraordinary extrasensory perception of the event, justice for Diana Goldston may never have come—and aside from putting a pair of murderers away for life, Carol Pate's work on this case has shown the world the reality of psychic detective work.

Ashley Howley's Post Mortem Psychic Reading

She was only 20 years old when she was last seen in 2004. And the sadness and despair of her family and friends was only heightened when her disappearance turned into a cold case.

The last the world had heard from Ashley Howley was a call she made to her local police department to report an instance of domestic violence. She claimed that her ex-boyfriend, 26-year-old Robert P. MacMichael, had assaulted her.

Shortly thereafter, she seemed to vanish without a trace. Her car, a gold-colored 1995 Pontiac Bonneville, was found abandoned in a parking lot, but there was no further information as to her whereabouts. The ex-boyfriend, MacMichael, was an obvious suspect, but without any clear evidence linking him to the disappearance, and without a body to indicate foul play, the case soon sank into a state of hopeless stagnation.

It was in the midst of this investigative malaise that none other than Ashley herself re-launched the investigation into her own death—or so self-proclaimed psychic detective Kristy Robinett would have us all believe. In one of the most unusual cases of all alleged psychic detective work, Robinett claims that she wasn't looking to solve a murder case—had in fact never heard of Ashley Howley or her disappearance—when Ashley's ghost came calling at her door!

Robinett says that it all began when she was startled awake in the middle of the night to see Ashley's spirit standing at the foot of her bed. Ashley's form was slightly greyish and translucent, and in Robinett's mind there was no question that this nighttime visitor was a ghost. And this ghost had a story to tell. The ghost of Ashley allegedly told Robinett that she had been "kidnapped and murdered."

Now, at this point in the investigation into Ashley's disappearance, everyone assumed that she was still alive. No one knew that she had been killed, yet Robinett was supposedly being supplied with this vital update in the case by the very spirit of the victim herself. Oddly enough, Robinett claims that the spirit didn't seem to have the wherewithal to supply its last name, only referring to itself to Ashley.

The visitation prompted Robinett to engage in a furious session with the Google search engine the following day. Having only the vaguest of hints to go on, Robinett typed "Ashley, missing, about 20 years old" into the Google search bar. And thanks to this miracle of modern technology, this was all she needed to know. The first page of her search results displayed a Crime Stoppers photo of a girl who was the exact likeness of the apparition she had seen the night before. Instantly knowing that this was the young woman who had met foul play, Robinett took full note of the name on her screen: Ashley Howley.

She scrolled down to the contact information for the site and immediately fired off an urgent e-mail to Crime Stoppers claiming to have vital information on the case. After being put into contact with Ashley's family, she learned of a nearby park that seemed to fit the impressions that Ashley's spirit was giving her. This psychic detective then teamed up with a park ranger to find the exact spot where she believed Ashley to be buried.

But before anyone moved to dig up the spot this psychic detective had so carefully picked out, her uncanny ability drew the attention of the police and resulted in her becoming a suspect herself. The authorities contacted her directly and demanded that she turn over her driver's license as they began to investigate her unusual knowledge regarding the circumstances of the case.

It turns out that Robinett's chosen spot had already been investigated by cadaver dogs. It had been determined that there might be a body buried in that location, but the area of interest bordered on private property. And not just any private property; this section of the park was actually linked to the private property of none other than Ashley's ex-boyfriend Robert P. MacMichael. The police had their suspicions, but were delaying an excavation of the spot until they could secure their prime suspect's permission to dig on the property.

Since the police had good reason to believe that Ashley's body might be buried in the park, they were incredibly suspicious when Robinett pointed out the very spot. Under normal circumstances no one not connected with the investigation should have had access to this kind of information—but little did the police know that they were dealing with a psychic detective!

As fate would have it, the ex-boyfriend's misdeeds caught up with him sooner rather than later. After murdering his mother and her boyfriend, the man fully confessed to all his crimes, and the police finally dug up Ashley's remains from the precise site that Kristy Robinett had pointed out. Ultimately, the efforts of this psychic detective pointed the way to the conviction of Ashley's killer, and Robert P. MacMichael was sentenced to three consecutive life sentences for the three lives he coldly snuffed out.

MacMichael showed little remorse for his crimes upon capture. In the years that he eluded authorities after Ashley's murder, he seems to have gotten the erroneous impression that he could get away with his atrocities. The method by which he had disposed of Ashley Howley bore testament to this hope. Her body was encased in concrete, as if the thick cement layers would be enough to hide his crimes—but all the cement in the world couldn't stop this psychic detective from finding the truth.

Tragedy at a Picnic

John Edward Futch and Cindy Rediger were high school sweethearts who did everything together. And so on the morning of January 5, 1978, when John asked Cindy to go on a picnic with him after school, she readily agreed. But long after the school day had ended, the friends and family of the pair had not heard anything from them. This was long before cell phones, so with no way to reach the couple, all anyone could do was wait.

At first it was speculated that the two had been in a bad traffic accident or some other such emergency situation. But the local hospitals—and even the county morgue—had no record of anyone resembling the ill-fated couple. After 24 hours had passed, investigators were actively seeking answers, and with no other leads to follow, the police went to John and Cindy's school to interview their peers.

They discovered that John and Cindy had mentioned that they might go to a local recreational area known as the "military trail" for their after-school picnic. This location was then vigorously searched for any signs of the couple, and soon investigators seemed to have found what they were looking for. They stumbled upon what appeared to be a hastily abandoned picnic, complete with a picnic blanket and scattered charcoal from a fire.

However, the investigators were dismayed to discover that there were no footprints anywhere near the site. The powdery sand prevalent in that region of Florida simply does not preserve this sort of forensic evidence. So the military trail had mostly grown cold, but there was still one aspect of the surroundings that stood out: a faded white house within eyesight of where John and Cindy had apparently had their picnic. This rental house was just across the street from the scene, so it seemed possible that the residents had seen something. But when investigators asked, they said they hadn't.

The slim hope that the young couple might still be alive was then dashed when John's car was found submerged in a nearby canal. It was now clear that that John and Cindy must have met a bitter end; as one of the investigators on the scene put it, "A hard-working kid like John doesn't just drive his car into a canal." Nevertheless, as ominous as the submerged vehicle was, there was still no sign of its former occupants. With no witnesses, no footprints, and no other leads to go on, investigators had hit a dead end.

This is when experienced psychic detective Phil Jordan entered the picture. Although many of the seasoned investigators scoffed at the notion of bringing a psychic onto their team, Jordan's previous success rate was so impressive that even the most ardent of skeptics could not easily dismiss him.

Jordan had famously proven the power of his psychic insight when a young boy named Tommy Kennedy had gone missing. Police had scoured the area for days without finding any sign of the boy, but after Tommy's father enlisted psychic detective Jordan's aid, he was able to visualize his precise location. As it turns out, Tommy had simply gotten lost, and as Jordan remotely viewed the scene in his mind, he saw the boy sound asleep underneath a tree. Jordan then drew a detailed map of the area that led police to that same tree Jordan had envisioned—where they did indeed find Tommy sleeping.

With a history of stunning results such as this—and with nothing else to go on—the skeptics grudgingly agreed to give Jordan a try. He was taken down to the assumed scene of the crime, where the picnic had taken place, in order to see what his extrasensory perception might be able to pick up. It came through loud and clear.

In his mind, Jordan could see the two happy lovers having a picnic together when they were suddenly interrupted by two men. The men were both armed, one with a rifle and the other with a shotgun. Jordan saw the men open fire on the couple—and then he drew a blank. The movie in his mind abruptly ended, but he was certain that they were both dead, shot execution-style in the head.

But if this was the case, the bodies had obviously been moved from the site of the killing. It was for this reason that Jordan was recruited, as he had been in so many other cases before: to use his special abilities to draw a detailed map of where he perceived the slain couple to have been taken.

Jordan's map took police down an old set of railroad tracks, past a sandy mound, and near an old white house—the very same house whose residents had already been questioned. Bolstered by Jordan's tips, investigators returned to the home, but upon their arrival they found the residence mysteriously abandoned. But although the occupants were gone, along with most of their belongings, interestingly enough, there was one item that they had left scattered throughout the house: shell casings.

They found a total of 22 shell casings, all of which could have come from a rifle similar to the one that Jordan had seen one of the men carrying in his vision. These casings were immediately collected and shipped off to a crime lab, and ballistics experts identified the rifle they came from as semiautomatic .22 Ruger. However, a search of the local gun shops didn't turn up any immediate matches, and without a match the casings were essentially useless.

Two months then went by, with the case at another standstill, before a bike rider made a gruesome discovery near the site where John and Cindy were believed to have been slain. Two bodies were found, and it did not take long to figure out that they were indeed the bodies of John and Cindy. It was now irrefutably clear that this tragic pair was no more.

When the bodies were examined, it was discovered that—just as psychic detective Jordan had maintained—the two had both been shot execution-style in the head. Bullets recovered from the bodies were tested and found to come from the same gun as the shell casings picked up at the neighboring house. But even though the bodies of the slain couple had been found, their killers were still on the loose.

Jordan redoubled his psychic efforts, and the visions he began to receive were startling in their depth. He kept picturing a man of Hispanic origin with dark hair and a mustache. He also intuited that this individual had a first name that began with the letter "A". (The tantalizingly incomplete nature of the information that psychics are able to provide sometimes boggles the mind, but for whatever reason this seems to be a recurring theme among psychic detectives.) To make Jordan's findings seem even more obscure, for some reason he kept seeing a recurring image of a dog—and something told him that the killer's dog would somehow play into the investigation. Jordan put all of these clues down on paper and turned them over to the police.

As investigators started to look into those clues, Jordan contacted a friend who did composite sketches for law enforcement and directed him to draw a picture of the man that his mind's eye saw. The resultant illustration showed the strikingly ominous visage of a man with dark eyes, high cheekbones, and a dark black mustache, just as Jordan envisioned. Jordan sent this illustration to investigators as well so they could search their photo database of offenders for any possible match.

Before a match could be found, however, they receive word that their suspects might have struck again. Another body had been discovered in the vicinity of the first crime, and it seemed to fit the same profile. A young woman named Laura Ann Gurney had been killed by an execution-style blast to the head from either a rifle or a shotgun.

The killer or killers were now on a real rampage, and authorities had barely even processed the Gurney crime scene before they struck again. The next victim was a young woman similar in appearance and background to Laura Ann Gurney and Cindy Rediger, and just like them she was sexually assaulted. The only difference was that she managed to get away, scaring her would-be murderer off the scene in the process. Crucially, she provided a detailed description of the attacker and his car.

Police then identified an offender who seemed to match the physical description given by both Jordan and the victim. This man also happened to have a first name that began with the letter "A", just as Jordan had predicted. His name was Adam Herrara, and he had a long criminal history. Herrara was placed in a photo lineup with other men of similar appearance, and the victim singled him out immediately.

Under the circumstances, police hoped for a confession; however, Adam Herrera was not going to be so obliging. Upon his subsequent arrest on charges of murder he hired a lawyer and stopped talking to detectives.

Shortly thereafter, investigators managed to contact his wife, Gloria. Amazingly, despite the considerable evidence of her husband's guilt, she initially tried to stand by his side. She was totally uncooperative at first, but after police stressed just how serious the charges were, she became a bit more talkative. Under interrogation, she finally said that her husband had admitted to her that he was involved in the murder of the two high school students. But according to Gloria, Herrera claimed that he wasn't the one who pulled the trigger.

Adam Herrera blamed everything on the other man he was with, a day laborer named Arnulfo Sanchez, claiming that he was the one who had shot John and then raped Cindy before killing her as well. According to this version of Herrera's story, he was just a "not-so-innocent bystander" who watched this base and vile brutality take place. Reserving judgment on the truth of this assertion, police immediately tracked down Sanchez and took him into custody for questioning.

Upon his own interrogation, Sanchez flipped the script and told a completely different story. Although Herrera had pointed the finger at him, Sanchez pointed it right back, claiming that Herrera had pulled the trigger. After listening to him and evaluating all of the evidence, authorities quietly determined that Adam Herrera appeared to be the guiltier of the two. They believed that he was simply trying to turn his accomplice into the fall guy for his crimes.

The prosecution therefore considered offering Sanchez a deal wherein he would receive a more lenient sentence if he testified against Adam Herrera. As it turned out, though, there was enough evidence against both men that no deals were necessary. They both plead guilty and received life without the possibility of parole. Psychic detective Phil Jordan's efforts on the case proved to be a critical factor in finally obtaining this justice for John and Cindy.

Andre Daigle's Last Night Out

Life isn't always what it seems, and 27-year-old Andre Daigle learned this the hard way. He was enjoying a night out with some friends at a Louisiana tavern called Mitchel's Lounge when he made the acquaintance of a beautiful woman. As he exchanged smiles with the pretty lady, it seemed like he was in for a great night. But as it turns this woman's beauty was only skin deep; her exquisite exterior masked the deviousness in her heart. Because after leaving with this beautiful stranger, Andre would never be seen again.

The first sign that Andre was in trouble came the next morning when he didn't show up for work. And while a lot of men do occasionally decide to ditch the Monday morning blues for an extended weekend, Andre just wasn't that kind of guy. He loved his job and always reported to work on time. So when he didn't punch in his time card that day, it was almost immediately suspected that something had gone awry.

When he couldn't be located or contacted, he was officially filed as a missing person. To their credit, investigators took the family's word that Andre's disappearance was highly unusual, and knowing that the first 48 hours are the most important when it comes to missing persons, they pulled out all the stops to locate him. The first thing they did was to retrace his footsteps. They found that the last person to see Andre that night was the friend with whom he'd been drinking that evening, a local kid named Nick Shelley.

Shelley told the police that he and Andre had parted company when Andre walked out of the bar with an unknown woman. He'd seen Andre and the woman get inside Andre's truck and drive off together. Other witnesses said that the woman's behavior had seemed somewhat odd; although Andre was a good-looking guy, to be sure, it struck them as strange just how eager this young woman was to get inside his truck.

Of course, if a trap had been set by this attractive lady it had already been sprung, and there was no going back. The lead investigator on the case, Detective Patrick Gallagher, decided to investigate this woman as thoroughly as possible and to speak to anyone who'd had any contact with her. Being that Andre had disappeared from a bar, Detective Gallagher naturally struck up a conversation with the bartender.

Fortunately for him, this lady and remembered the night of Andre's disappearance quite clearly. She recalled seeing Andre and the mystery woman talking quite amicably with each other. She was able to give a detailed description of the event and the woman herself. Time was now of the essence, and with the chances of finding Andre alive and unharmed getting slimmer by the hour, Detective Gallagher took his gut instinct that something was terribly wrong and put it to work.

An investigative team was quickly launched to scour the area. They searched through just about every square inch of the city and surrounding area in order to locate the missing man, but were not able to find any trace of Andre whatsoever.

Growing more and more frustrated and worried, the Daigle family reached out to a local psychic by the name of Rosemarie Kerr. In their first meeting with the psychic, the family gave her a photo of Andre and simply asked her to tell them what she saw.

As soon as Rosemarie Kerr touched the photograph, she exclaimed that something "terrible" had occurred. In her mind's eye, she began to see a hammer coming down on Andre's head and felt a tremendous burning pain in the same region of her own skull. She then envisioned a map of the entire suburb of Slidell, a suburb of New Orleans, and perceived Andre's truck being driven in this region in real time. She then abruptly instructed the family to "go quick" to see if they could spot this truck.

Andre's brothers didn't waste any time. They hopped into a car and raced to the location the psychic claimed to have seen in her vision. Incredibly enough, right as they got on the exit to head toward Slidell, they saw Andre's truck passing right in front of them. It was unmistakably his vehicle—the license plate number matched—but when they looked inside the windows they didn't see Andre. Instead, they saw a couple of men they don't know.

The brothers decided to follow the truck, and their pursuit quickly became a high-speed chase, at times reaching over 90 miles an hour. In the middle of this desperate race they came across a police car on patrol, whereupon they pulled over and manage to explain the situation to Officer Tom Corley. Aware of Andre's case, the patrolman agreed to join the chase.

The pursuit only ended when they cornered the truck on a dead-end road. Leaping from his squad car, Officer Corley raised his gun and ordered the cornered men to exit their vehicle. Realizing that they were trapped, the men finally gave up. After they were safely handcuffed and thrown in the back of his cruiser, Officer Corley inspected the truck.

Inside, he found several weapons, as well as a bunch of receipts from pawn shops. It would later be determined that these receipts were all for property stolen from Andre that the criminals had hawked to pawn brokers. But since the full extent of their crimes could not yet be proven, the men were initially brought in on "suspicion of traffic violations" and "auto theft." Aside from their names—Charles Gervais and Michael Philips—so far, all that could be determined about these crooks was that they had been caught red-handed with a missing man's truck.

But if anyone had hoped that Gervais and Philips would quickly admit to having a hand in Andre's disappearance and presumed murder, they were sorely disappointed. The only thing they admitted was the obvious fact that they were driving a stolen truck; everything else, including how they had received that piece of stolen property, they kept between themselves.

As a result, the investigation into what had happened to Andre hit another delay. The investigators tore through Andre's truck and the suspects' apartment, but they still couldn't find even the slightest clue. With no evidence directly linking Gervais and Philips to Andre, the men's story that they had simply acquired an abandoned truck and knew nothing about Andre's disappearance could not be disproven.

Detectives felt like they were back on square one, and accordingly they went right back to the basics. They questioned all the people who might possibly have encountered Andre during the fateful night of his disappearance. They also asked the bar's patrons and employees to let them know if the mystery woman ever returned.

Soon after this request was made, the bartender made a late-night phone call to the police station when she thought she saw the femme fatale in the bar. But after the cops rushed over to confront the woman, it became clear that the bartender's tip was nothing more than a case of mistaken identity. This dead end was followed by several days of similarly fruitless false leads.

Unable to find answers on their own, investigators began to consider going back to the person who had led them to the first major break in the case psychic detective Rosemarie Kerr. It was Kerr, after all, who had led them to Andre's pickup truck, and that fact made it much easier to consider such unorthodox investigative methodology. They arranged to meet the psychic detective at the bar from which Andre had disappeared.

As soon as she entered the room, she felt impressions and vibrations from the night that Andre vanished. As she stood in front of one of the pool tables, she felt the distinct impression that Andre had played pool at that table that night. She then moved her perception of events outside of the bar and began to perceive Andre being taken (or directed) to travel near a body of water of some sort and a set of railroad tracks. She also kept sensing the number 7. This number was somehow important, perhaps related to the location Andre was being taken to, and she couldn't shake it from her mind.

As she concentrated on this number, she began to feel that all the air had been sucked out of her lungs. It seemed like she could no longer breathe, like she was suffocating, as she envisioned these events. The psychic then took a deep breath and dramatically announced for all to hear that Andre was no more. She had just witnessed his death through her extrasensory perception. She reported that this unfortunate soul had already passed on "to the light." This psychic detective then informed investigators that two males and a female had been directly involved in his demise. The police took this information for whatever they thought it was worth and continued their investigation of the case.

They soon discovered that Charles Gervais and Michael Philips had not lived in the apartment they had recently searched for very long. They had been evicted from a previous residence shortly beforehand—and oddly enough, the apartment number of this previous residence was 7, just like Rosemarie had envisioned.

Armed with this knowledge, they were able to secure a search warrant for these premises. What they uncovered would only serve to verify what the psychic detective had reported—and what Andre's family had feared. They found a large bloodstain underneath the carpet, which was a clear indication that someone had been struck with a blunt object and subsequently lost a lot of blood. Samples of this blood were sent off to a lab and tested, and the police soon received confirmation that the blood did indeed belong to Andre Daigle.

With the evidence mounting against them, the suspects were finally convinced to confess to their role in the crime. Charles Gervais and Michael Philips admitted to beating Andre to death with a hammer and strangling him before disposing of his body in a local swamp. The fact that psychic detective Rosemarie Kerr had envisioned Andre suffocating just before he died seemed to back this story up.

But what about the mystery woman who had led Andre to his death in the first place? Who was she? Her name was Thelma Horne, and apparently Gervais and Philips had regularly been using her to attract men back to their apartment so that they could ambush them.

After confessing, the men led detectives to where they had disposed of Andre Daigle. As if they were reading from a script laid down by the premonitions of the psychic detective, the suspects directed them down the interstate to exit number 7, once again bringing up the number that had been reverberating so clearly in Rosemarie Kerr's mind. Here in the brush underneath a bridge, they finally found Andre Daigle's mangled corpse packed up in a cardboard box as if he were nothing more than a pile of rubbish.

But Andre was much more than that; he was a young man with hopes and dreams that were tragically dashed by senseless violence. He had his whole life ahead of him before a trio of malcontents and miscreants took it away. All three of these villains were brought to trial for first degree murder. And in case anyone still had any doubts, the psychic detective Rosemarie Kerr was brought in to testify in order to dispel them. As a result of her extraordinary efforts, all three of these murderous conspirators were found guilty and sentenced to life without the possibility of parole.

The Jewel Thief

In the affluent suburbs of Miami, Florida, a wealthy attorney named Herb and his wife Barbara were woken in the middle of the night by the sound of someone making a commotion inside their home. Their first thought was that it was their young son, but they soon learned otherwise when they heard in the darkness the words, "Shut up or I'll kill you."

The couple was apparently being robbed. They were tied up while a burglar ransacked the place. Several hours after he left, Herb and Barbara managed to free themselves—but after they went to check on their children, they were horrified to find that their 18-year-old daughter Erin was missing. She had just come home from college for a visit, and now she was gone. Even more disturbing was the bloodstain found on her bed.

You can call it a gut feeling, or a policeman's own latent psychic intuition, but investigators felt early on that this crime was not random. They believed that the perpetrator was familiar with the family. Their first person of interest was Erin's boyfriend, Mike Devito. However, Mike appeared to be just as shocked and distraught about what had happened as everyone else. His genuine dismay—coupled with his airtight alibi—soon convinced detectives to scratch him off the list of suspects.

Soon thereafter, investigators were tipped off to a grisly scene. Herb and Barbara's Mercedes Benz, which had been stolen by the intruder, was found abandoned—and the body of young Erin was discovered inside the car. It appeared that the whole crime scene had been staged, and the perpetrator had morbidly posed Erin inside the vehicle.

She was wrapped up in blankets and had four stab wounds on her body, but the massive amount of blood that these wounds would have produced was not present in the vehicle. There was only a small amount of blood on the seat next to her body, which clearly indicated that Erin had bled out elsewhere. After making this gruesome find, investigators canvassed the entire region, knocking on doors and asking if anyone had heard or seen anything unusual in the past few days.

They were hoping against hope that someone had witnessed either the murder itself or at least the killer dropping off Erin's body. But their investigation produced few leads—until, that is, they knocked on a door a little closer to home. As it turned out, Herb and Barbara's next-door neighbor had indeed seen something of note. Shortly before Erin's disappearance, the neighbor had seen her with a man she hadn't recognized.

This was a tantalizing piece of evidence opening the door to a new suspect in the case, but without any further information there was no way for the detectives to pursue the new lead. It was at this point that they made the acquaintance of a psychic detective named Micki Dahne. As is usually the case, many of the investigators were quite skeptical about enlisting the aid of a psychic, but since Dahne's reputation preceded her, they allowed her to come aboard.

They had Dahne visit Erin's home to see if she could get any impressions from the surroundings. An as soon as Dahne entered Erin's room, she started to feel something and knew that she was on the right track. (Like many psychics, Dahne finds it easier to get in tune with her subject if she is in the living space they once occupied. It also helps her to get acquainted with objects that belonged to the target of her ESP.)

As Micki looked around Erin's room, the object that seemed to reverberate the most was one of Erin's old notebooks. As soon as she picked it up and ran her hand across its front, she began to receive a massive torrent of information about what had befallen the teenager. She could hear Erin literally screaming at her, "Boyfriend… it was my boyfriend!"

Micki had the clear impression that whoever had killed Erin was someone that she had known on an intimate level. She felt that, although Erin had dated several guys, this man was someone who was at the top of her list. As interesting as this bit of information was, however, police needed a little bit more than vague hints of the murdered girl's secret crushes.

They pushed Micki to see what else she could get. After much concentration and focus on this man that Erin seemed so interested in, she could perceive that he worked with his hands, somewhere around water. She then began to perceive the letters

"RS", and she knew that they were the man's initials. As is often the case with psychic premonitions, while the full name eluded her, the initials "RS" seemed to scream out at her at top volume.

This information would prove important when a local pawn broker was found to have some of the jewelry that had been stolen from the residence. The owner of the pawn shop had dealt with a man who attempted to sell him the jewelry without a photo ID. The owner refused, since by law a photo ID was required to sell items to a pawn shop. The man left after he was informed of this, but promptly returned with an elderly lady who had been waiting outside in his car.

This woman, Holly Sandborn, was apparently the man's mother. She was the one who finally produced an ID so that the jewelry could be sold. This proved to be the link that the cops needed in order to put a face and a full name to Micki Dahne's psychic vision of RS. Through the address on the photocopy the pawn broker had made of her driver's license, they were able to track Holly Sandborn down.

When accused of helping her son pawn stolen jewelry, Mrs. Sandborn at first played dumb and pretended that she knew nothing about any jewelry. But the detectives soon ran out of patience with that story. Impressing upon her just how serious the situation was, they convinced her to admit that she had indeed helped her son, Russel Sandborn, pawn the jewelry.

Back at the police department, they ran a background check on Russel Sandborn. Quite a few red flags emerged immediately. Russel turned out to be an ex-con with a long rap sheet, making it entirely conceivable that he could be the killer.

As police were waiting for a warrant to search Sandborn's apartment, they heard from psychic detective Micki Dahne again. Micki informed them that she kept having premonitions of some sort of hand-written letter from the killer that would prove his guilt. This was another revelation from the psychic that would prove to be pivotal in the case. Micki also revealed that she had been having visions of Erin being attacked on the beach, saying that she believed that more evidence would be found on the beach.

When police gained entry into Sandborn's apartment, they noticed a section of the carpet that—although thoroughly clean—seemed unusually stiff. They then cut this section out and found bloodstains. Strangely enough, they also found a hand-written letter addressed to one of Sandborn's ex-cellmates. The contents of this missive to his prison buddy couldn't have been more incriminating.

The letter discussed how Sandborn had met a beautiful woman with rich parents—and how he had robbed them. This was an obvious description of Erin and her wealthy father and mother Herb and Barbara. With this incredibly incriminating letter to back them up, detectives turned up the heat on Sandborn's mother to provide the man's whereabouts. Cracking under the pressure, she told them that they would find him on the beach.

True to Micki's vision, Russel Sandborn, the RS of her nightmarish visions, was hiding out at a motel on the beach. After stopping by the lobby for Russel's room number and a master key, the police entered his room with guns drawn. But Russel wasn't there. They pulled back and set up a stakeout, and when Russel Sandborn returned to the motel a few hours later, they swarmed in to arrest him.

If Russel was surprised, he didn't act like it. Just like the visions of the psychic detective who had helped bring him to justice, Russel Sandborn's own guilty conscience had apparently provided him with a premonition of his impending incarceration. If so, he wasn't disappointed. After standing trial, he was given what prosecutors like to refer to as a "Buck Rogers" sentence, meaning that he'll be able to get out of prison sometime in the 25th century!

The Psychic Gamble

It was only early April, but the humid air of Gonzales, Louisiana, felt like summer. It made those in attendance at the gathering of a local church group uneasy—and their unease was only compounded when one of their most faithful members failed to show up for the service. Her name was Lilian Philopy, and her fellow parishioners were quick to notify authorities that something was very wrong.

Unfortunately, their fears proved to be well founded. A police courtesy check revealed that Lilian had been viciously murdered in her own home. She was found sprawled on the floor of her master bedroom with a blanket partially covering her body—as if the killer thought that a flimsy bedspread would be enough to hide his heinous crime! Lifting those bloodstained covers immediately revealed the truth. Lilian had been repeatedly stabbed in the neck and chest.

And to add insult to injury, the murder weapon was none other than her own kitchen knife. It was obvious that whoever had done this horrible deed had some degree of familiarity with Lilian's home. But the scene also fit a troubling pattern that had become established over the past six months throughout the greater Louisiana region. Lilian was the third known victim of a series of similarly perpetrated crimes. Residents had begun to whisper fearfully among themselves that they had a serial killer on their hands.

As investigators probed the crime scene further, they discovered that the killer had gained entrance into Lilian's home by putting a chair on top of an outside air-conditioning unit and climbing through an attic vent. The only evidence that he left behind was a telltale shoe print on the roof.

Short of demanding that every Louisiana resident submit their shoe prints for comparison to the one left behind at Lilian's residence, the police had little to go on. It was during this deadlock that veteran psychic detective Rose Kopp came onto the scene. Stressing her experience, Rose was able to convince the chief of police, Bill Landry, to let her lend her aid.

Focusing upon the crime scene, Rose meditated until her mind traveled back in time to the crime itself. In her mind's eye, Rose saw a man wielding a knife lurking in Lilian's home. She then saw the man go into Lilian's room, catch her by surprise, and begin to stab her viciously in the face, neck and chest. Rose was able to gather a lot of information from this vision; she could rewind and even freeze-frame the images to give her a better idea of what she was seeing.

From this vantage point, she could ascertain that the attacker was 5-foot-10 and had the calloused hands of a laborer. But for all of her clairvoyant ability to send her mind back in time, she was unable to illuminate the darkness that the crime scene was shrouded in, and the actual face of the perpetrator still remained unclear to her. Nevertheless, as ambiguous as some of the details were, Bill Landry was ready to take any lead on the case that he could get.

The killer, however, did not wait for Chief Landry to make use of the new data that psychic detective Rose Kopp had provided for him. There was yet another slaying in Louisiana that featured the same kind of forced entry and the slaying of the victim with a household item. Rose wanted to stop this killer as badly as anyone else, so she refocused her efforts and concentrated on the perpetrator of these crimes.

In her clairvoyant sessions she envisioned something which at the outset seemed rather odd: the impression of a river and the image of a rat. She also kept perceiving an old woman's hand drawing out the words 'River Rat" over and over. What relation these two things could have to the suspect was at first unclear even to her. As she was mulling it over, Chief Landry offered to bring her to the crime scene in person to see if she could perceive anything else about the case.

Her mind immediately traveled back to the time of the crime, and she saw the suspect placing a wrought iron chair on top of the AC unit right before he made his forced entry into Lilian's home. But this time, instead of just focusing on this man, she managed to look behind him and see a car parked on the side of the road a short distance away. It was a four-door sedan, and inside was a fat blonde woman who seemed to be waiting for the suspect to finish his mischief.

The psychic detective then refined her vision even more and zoomed in on the passenger seat and floor of the car. She saw bits of paper strewn all over the interior. As she focused in on these pieces of paper, she realized that they were gambling receipts. It's not clear if this psychic just happened to have a penchant for gambling and knew what to look for, or if the psychic impression itself told her what the pieces of paper were, but whatever the case, she came away from the experience absolutely positive that the papers she saw were associated with gambling and that the suspect had a real gambling problem motivating him to commit his crimes. Without any other good motive in sight, the police began to work this angle to see if it would pan out, but they made very little headway.

The department soon got another early morning phone call reporting the killer's latest attack. The situation appeared the same as the others, with the victims being elderly and their attacker apparently a criminal opportunist who already knew them. But there was one difference between this case and the others: these would-be murder victims survived! It was from the female survivor that the clearest description emerged. She said that the attacker was a slender white man of approximately 35 years of age. All of this seemed to fit the psychic detective's description fairly well.

For her part, Rose conducted another remote viewing session, this time focusing more on the accomplice. As she focused on her, she could now see the woman working at a diner, pouring coffee, serving food, and carrying dishes back to the kitchen. Determined to identify this woman, Rose zeroed in on her name tag—and astonishingly enough, she was able to see it perfectly. This was no mere set of initials or other vague intimation; she clearly saw the name Cindy emblazoned on that name tag. With the woman's first name established, Rose peered out the window of the diner where the accomplice worked. From this vantage point she could see a billboard with a cow on it right out front. This billboard bovine became burned into her mind as an important landmark on the murderers' trail.

Meanwhile, the canvassing campaign of the local casinos had finally gotten a response. The task force was tipped off to a man who'd gone from wagering very small amounts of money and being broke all the time to becoming a big and extravagant spender seemingly overnight. Reports of this man's sudden transformation piqued the interest of those handling the case, and after sifting through the records they were able to identify him as a local gambler by the name of Daniel Blank. Blank fit the description given by Rose and the surviving witness perfectly He was about 35, was a white male, and seemed to have a real problem with losing money at the casinos.

Investigators also discovered that Blank had a girlfriend named Cindy. Now they just needed to locate her. Harkening back to Rose's vision of the cow billboard, they began scouring the area in search of this odd landmark. They did find one near a long-shuttered meat processing plant, but were unable to locate either the diner or Cindy herself.

Meanwhile, they were taking a good, long look at Daniel Blank and his possible motive for the crimes. By this point they were very much sold on the theory that Daniel had murdered simply to get money for his gambling habit, and as soon as they had enough information to go forward, they set out to track him down. They eventually caught up with him in Texas.

In police custody some of the more humanizing aspects of the killer's personality began to emerge, and detectives were quick to exploit these emotional fault lines in order to get answers. They knew that Blank's mother had recently passed away, and they brought it up during an interrogation. When they did, the suspect's mood changed entirely and he became very emotional. Sensing that he was flustered, the detectives began asking him about the jewelry that had been stolen and what he'd done with the money. As they continued to hammer away at him, the emotionally overwhelmed Blank cracked and started revealing details about the crime that no one but the killer would have known.

Before the night was over the police had a full confession. Blank had known all of his victims personally. Some of them he had worked for, some of them he had become acquainted with through some other avenue, but none of them were strangers; he knew them all. Investigators even discovered that these people that he knew and was friendly with had given him a nickname. They called him "River Rat."

The odds of Rose Kopp coming up with this name at random are astronomically high, so this detail seems to be clear evidence of her prowess as a psychic detective. As a result of this extrasensory extra help, Daniel Blank was tried and convicted of murder. He is currently sitting on death row at a prison in Angola, Louisiana.

The Party Gone Bad

A young woman named Nicole Arochas had her parents very concerned when she went to a party and didn't return the next day. No matter the situation, Nicole always checked in with her parents, and so Nicole's mother had a gut feeling that something just wasn't right. She called 911 to report her daughter's disappearance, and the police immediately began an investigation.

The first thing they asked was what kind of vehicle Nicole drove. (This is standard procedure in such cases, because it allows police to run checks to see if the missing person's car has been towed away or impounded somewhere in the middle of the night.) They then checked with nearby jails, hospitals, and even morgues to see if Nicole had found herself inside any of these facilities following her late-night partying. With these official avenues explored and scratched off their list, investigators began looking into those who knew Nicole on a personal level.

They reached out to all of her peers, and especially those who had been with her during the party, to see if any of them knew her whereabouts or had witnessed anything unusual. All of her friends put up a stone wall of silence, however, maintaining that as far as they could tell Nicole was having a wonderful time at the party and had left in a good state of mind. After surveying the party house where Nicole Arochas was last seen, however, police were not exactly convinced that this testimony could be trusted.

They found a wrecked home with beer bottles strewn everywhere and ashtrays full of cigarettes and drug paraphernalia. They knew that if the house looked this bad during an official police investigation, it must have looked 10 times worse before. It was a total flophouse, and the party hadn't been contained inside the four walls of the dilapidated home either. Detectives stepped outside to find a literal trail of beer bottles and other party debris leading all the way to a set of railroad tracks behind the home.

But as much of a mess as these merrymakers had created in their home and in the neighboring area, police could not pinpoint any sign of foul play that might have led to the disappearance of Nicole Arochas. They searched the woods nearby and peered into embankments and side roads hoping to find a sign of Nicole or her car, but turned up nothing.

As is so often the case with these accounts, it was when they had reached an absolute dead end that the standard-issue police detectives found themselves reaching out to a detective of a whole other caliber—a psychic detective named Frank St. James.

St. James was already a 30-year veteran in the field when he was recruited to sort out the facts of the disappearance of Nicole Arochas. To begin his extrasensory fact-finding mission, St. James was given a photo of Nicole so that he could "tune in" to her spirit and gain an impression of what she had gone through the night of the party. Putting himself literally in the mind of Nicole during those moments, St. James was able to perceive the house in which the party had taken place and the railroad tracks behind it—even though no one had told him about either one.

Even more incredibly, he also perceived the friends who were with Nicole at the party that night and began to list them off by name. Without any prior knowledge and no way of knowing save for his psychic gifts, he started spouting off her acquaintances: "James… Lauren… Michael…" But there was also a more mysterious individual that he couldn't put a name to. He didn't know who this dark figure was, but Frank St. James sensed that he had something to do with Nicole's disappearance.

In the middle of his vision, St. James suddenly felt like everything around him was spinning. He felt like he was losing control—and even more ominously, he felt that someone was menacing Nicole in the midst of this turmoil. He then picked up a man whose name he intuited to be Rick. He saw this man with dark, shaggy hair and believed him to be a real threat to Nicole.

Armed with this information, police decided to have another crack at interviewing Nicole's peers. They put her friends through another battery of interviews, hoping to break down the wall of silence that surrounded Nicole's disappearance by questioning them about the mysterious and menacing man that St. James had picked up. This finally seemed to hit a nerve, and now Nicole's friends divulged some new details. They admitted that Nicole's ex-boyfriend was present at the party, and that perhaps there had been some tension between the two.

With this tantalizing new lead in hand, police rushed to the residence of Nicole's ex-boyfriend. They had no idea what they might find there; it was entirely possible that Nicole had made up with the man and was staying at his home voluntarily, but on the other hand, he might be holding her hostage. So it was that the cops showed up at his door with open minds—but with guns drawn—to find some answers.

At first, the ex-boyfriend struck investigators as suspicious due to his high level of defensiveness. Nevertheless, he was completely open to a search of his residence, and upon further inquiry he seemed to have absolutely nothing to hide. After a thorough interview and walkthrough of his home, it was determined that he most likely had nothing at all to do with Nicole's disappearance.

Having hit another brick wall, police once again paid a visit to psychic detective Frank St. James. This time they took him directly to the putative scene of the crime—if there in fact was a crime—at the party house. As St. James walked around the home, he was immediately struck by a feeling akin to deja vu. It's a feeling that many psychics and other intuitive individuals recognize, in which they experience what should be unknown surroundings on a familiar basis, as if they have been there before.

St. James was moving around the rooms of the house searching for answers when he felt himself getting drawn into one particular section. Here he got the sensation that Nicole was attempting to communicate with him directly. As he attempted to tune in to her communication, St. James began to feel his heart flutter within his chest, and he realized that this was the same sensation that Nicole had experienced the night of the party.

For whatever reason, her health was deteriorating and she was in mortal danger. St. James felt her fear as he saw her being led to a red car and a black car. He perceived that the black car was Nicole's, while the red car was being used by the other individuals as an escort. She was being taken to her car, but she was not the one driving it. St. James was then compelled to go outside and walk along the railroad tracks. Here he received another direct impression of Nicole: Her black car was parked a short distance from the tracks. It was hidden off to the side near some trees, behind cattails, and underneath a bridge with one of its wheels submerged deep in the ground.

From all of these details that Nicole seemed to be downloading right into St. James's mind, he was able to draw a detailed map and hand it off to the police. A search party was raised and sent to the exact location that St. James had outlined in his map.

Just as the psychic detective had envisioned, Nicole's black car was discovered partially submerged in the mud, underneath a bridge near the woods, surrounded by a wild growth of cattails. As they neared the car, a much more horrifying scene revealed itself as they identified the dead body of Nicole Arochas slumped over in the seat. There did not seem to be any obvious trauma on the body, and with the cause of death unclear, it became an urgent matter to preserve her body and send it for autopsy immediately.

The medical examiner who performed the autopsy determined that Nicole had died of a heart attack after a drug overdose. This led to initial speculation that the young woman had committed suicide. However, when investigators found that she had no history of depression or suicidal ideation, they concluded that it was improbable that she would have left a party that she seemed to be enjoying in order to overdose on drugs and end her life.

The suicide theory was furthermore debunked by the fact that there were no syringes or any other drug paraphernalia in the vehicle. Whatever had happened to Nicole had apparently happened before she and her car ended up half submerged under a bridge. This was confirmed by tests showing that Nicole was so loaded up on drugs that she would have been unable to drive her car to get there. In other words, she had been driven there by someone else, who had then left her there to die.

With the evidence suggesting some sort of foul play mounting, the police went back to the witnesses at the party and attempted to break through their conspiracy of silence once more. These further interrogations of the last people to have seen Nicole alive—her supposed friends, no less—finally produced some results.

Her peers finally admitted that Nicole had left the party in quite questionable condition accompanied by a young man named Michael Reed. According to them, Reed, Nicole and two other friends left the house, and shortly thereafter Reed injected Nicole with some sort of drug. Nicole had an almost immediate adverse reaction to the substance and went into cardiac arrest.

Unable to revive her, the group panicked. Wishing to escape blame for her death, they concocted the harebrained scheme of loading up Nicole's body and driving her car—presumably followed by the red car that St. James had envisioned—to the sandy embankment underneath the nearby bridge. Concerned only with avoiding trouble for themselves, the group then callously positioned Nicole's corpse in her vehicle in the hope that if it was discovered, it would look like she had died alone by her own hand.

Nicole did willingly take the drugs that Reed injected her with. But Reed was the one who had purchased the illegal drugs, and furthermore he had sought to hide Nicole's body and tamper with her corpse. By these actions he opened himself up to multiple felony charges. He was arrested and convicted for his crimes, and as a result the parents of Nicole Arochas were finally able to get closure and justice for their beloved daughter. The clues that led to the resolution of this case may have been brought forth in an unorthodox manner, but the results achieved by this psychic detective were about as solid as could be.

The Baton Rouge Serial Killer

For 10 years, southern Louisiana had been preyed upon by a man who had become known as the Baton Rouge Serial Killer. This murderer victimized women in the greater Baton Rouge area, breaking into their homes, raping, beating and strangling them, and slitting their throats. Fear of this unknown assailant was already at a fever pitch in 1998 when a neighbor asked police to check on 28-year-old Randi Mebruer.

Although there was no forced entry, it was a horrible scene that the officers came upon. The house was completely ransacked, and there was blood all over the place. From the condition of the bed, it was obvious that a sexual assault had taken place. But Randi Mebruer was nowhere to be seen. Investigators feared the worst, but they really didn't know if she was still alive or not.

They immediately began to canvass the area for any clue as to her whereabouts. They interviewed all of her neighbors and searched the neighborhood thoroughly, but they couldn't turn up any leads. Meanwhile, two other women were found murdered in their home not far away. DNA retrieved from these two victims was found to belong to the Baton Rouge Serial Killer. Police quickly connected the dots and concluded that these two murders, perpetrated in the same general area and around the same time, were linked to the disappearance of Randi Mebruer.

The mother of one of the victims, Ann Pace, was determined to find out what happened to her daughter, Charlotte Murray Pace. Desperate for answers, she contacted Anne Williams a local forensics consultant, hoping that she could find some clue as to what had befallen her daughter. But Anne Williams, with all of her scientific expertise in forensics, opted to consult with someone who used methods of a whole other order: psychic detective Jeanne Borgen.

Borgen, a veteran in the field, had narrowed down the process of "tuning in" to her telepathic targets to focus on just three main pieces of information. To get started. all she needed was the victim's name, date of birth, and the last place they were seen. From this miniscule amount of data, she could begin to latch onto her target and gather information. She was able to see through their eyes and witness what had happened to them at a particular moment in time. Like many other psychic detectives, once she zeroed in on that person's identity and last known location, she could experience their last few moments first hand.

When Borgen attuned herself to Charlotte Murray Pace in this fashion, she beheld a clear picture of the events that had led to her demise. First, she witnessed an earlier encounter with the man responsible for Pace's death. As he hung around her neighborhood, the man tried to strike up a conversation, but

Pace, sensing that something wasn't right, rebuffed his overtures. Borgen got the impression that this man wanted to get inside Pace's house but Pace wouldn't let him in.

The image was as clear as day, and Borgen could see the man's face in great detail as he stalked Pace's house. According to her mental notes, he had hard, chiseled features, light brown skin, and dark hair. She perceived his height to be about six feet.

Then her mind moved to a truly horrifying scene. The man had broken into Pace's home, and the psychic could see him standing right in front of her immediately before he lunged to attack her. With a sense of great urgency, Borgen relayed this information to forensics expert Anne Williams.

No sooner had she done so than she began getting mental flashes of another woman whom she perceived to be the killer's next intended victim. She saw an attractive young lady in her mid-20s with long dark hair. She sensed that the killer was stalking this woman intently, having already decided to attack her. She saw her residence between two big trees, and she got the impression that there was some feature of the environment that involved "whiskey."

The details were incredibly vague, but Borgen frantically supplied them to police in the hope that they could prevent another woman from meeting such a tragic end. But before anyone could even begin to figure out what the psychic detective's information might mean, they were waylaid with the news of another victim. She was a beautiful young Louisiana State University student, in her mid-20s, with long dark black hair, just as Borgen had foreseen. Her name was Carrie Lynn Yoder, and she was the Baton Rouge Serial Killer's next victim. Another stunning revelation was that Yoder's body was recovered from a body of water just off Interstate 10 called Whiskey Bay. It was an uncanny match for the other clue that Borgen had intuited, that the crime would be associated with the word "whiskey."

With this gruesome discovery the story of the slain LSU student gained considerable traction in the local news, and after the ensuing public outcry, a task force was put together to track the suspect down. Police initially put out a profile of the suspect suggesting that he was most likely a physically fit white male who worked in construction or some similar field. But Jeanne Borgen, the psychic member of the task force, begged to differ. It was clear in her mind that the suspect was an African American man who was stalking the area. But with no corroboration of Borgen's psychic impressions, the task force continued with their theory of a lean, fit serial killer of European ancestry.

They thought they had hit pay dirt when a man named Shannon Kohler is taken in under suspicious circumstances. Kohler seemed to fit the profile; he earned his living as a welder and a laborer, he was physically fit, a bit of a loner, and he was a European American. But a DNA swab of his mouth conclusively ruled him out as the Baton Rouge Serial Killer. The incident showed just how far investigators were from solving the case, and Kohler would later file a lawsuit seeking damages for his detention and the forcible seizure of his DNA.

In the meantime, the task force cut their losses and finally admitted that they needed to change course. That decision brought them back to the dogged psychic detective who had followed the case from the beginning: Jeanne Borgen. The lead detective on the case, Lieutenant David MacDavid, began the effort by inviting her out to the crime scene at Whiskey Bay.

Walking along the bay, Borgen again envisioned the killer, and she saw the same man with light brown skin, low-set eyes, and thick mustache. She saw him staring through windows looking for victims, and she got the feeling that this man was a serial peeping Tom who had been peering into houses like this since his childhood. Borgen's peeping Tom theory became the next major lead in the case, and investigators began to search through their arrest records for a man with a history of such nefarious activity.

In the meantime, Borgen got to work with forensic expert Anne Williams on a composite sketch of the man she was seeing in her mind. Using the latest forensic computer program, they came up with a detailed composite of the suspect just as Borgen envisioned him. They immediately fired this composite off to Lieutenant MacDavid. When he saw it, he was shocked. He was sure that he had seen this man before.

When he pulled up the arrest records of peeping Toms he had been compiling, he found the man at the top of the list. His name was Derrick Todd Lee, and he had a long history of criminal offenses ranging from peeping into people's windows to break-ins and burglaries. His mug shot seemed to be a nearly perfect match to the composite drawing produced by Borgen and Williams.

Even the most skeptical of detectives could not have ignored these coincidences; was a lead too good to pass up. So investigators immediately looked into Lee's personal timeline so see where he may have been at the times of the Baton Rouge Serial Killer murders. In the process, MacDavid was able to gather enough circumstantial evidence for a warrant ordering that a DNA swab be obtained from Derrick Todd Lee.

When a positive hit came back, they knew they finally had their man. Derrick Todd Lee was tried and convicted of murder in 2003, and has since died in prison, passing away from an undisclosed medical condition in 2016. Derrick Todd Lee, like his victims, has passed on over to the other side. Whether his punishment for his misdeeds continues in the afterlife is between him and his Creator, but the folks in Louisiana are no doubt sleeping a little bit easier knowing that the specter of the Baton Rouge Serial Killer can haunt them no more.

Running from Justice

After a prison break in Louisiana, dangerous convicts Billy Wilson and Roy Moore had been traveling across the state leaving a trail of terror in their wake. The authorities had set up road blocks to intercept the inmates, but they had somehow slipped past them and were now ranging far and wide. But little did these two villains know that they were heading straight for one of the most prolific psychic detectives in the land, and she was ready for them!

Joyce Morgan had a history of accurate predictions and premonitions, and before the information was even released to the public she knew about the breakout—and she knew that the men were headed her way. She followed the inmates' progress in her mind's eye as they fled from justice. At this point she didn't even know who the escapees were, but she could clearly see their faces in her mind, and she could clearly perceive that they were up to no good. And she was most certainly right. The men had stolen a pickup truck and were racing up the highway in a northwesterly direction, robbing and pillaging along the way.

Morgan also had the inexplicable impression of the letters "Y-O-U" repeating over and over again. This psychic detective was completely overwhelmed by what she was experiencing, but she felt that she didn't have enough information to go to the police. She knew that police are a generally skeptical bunch, and with such vague murmurings as she was experiencing she figured that they would ignore her. Little did she know, however, that she was hitting many of the details of the escape in Louisiana right on the head. That being the case, authorities just might have viewed her as an important resource from the very beginning. But at any rate, she decided to stay quiet for the time being.

In the meantime, the danger the two men posed grew even more ominous after a local mother called 911 to report that her daughter was missing. Jennifer Barton had been outside playing with her brother when an unknown pickup truck pulled up, abducted her in broad daylight right in front of her house, and left the scene with her. Her brother had seen everything, but all he could say was that the truck was green. Others in the close-knit community were able to provide more details, however; since it was a small town where everyone knew everyone else, this strange truck had stuck out like a sore thumb.

Authorities quickly latched onto this information. They knew that finding the truck would be the key to finding Jennifer Barton, so they sent out an all points bulletin describing the vehicle in great detail. Pretty soon they received their lead. A truck that matched the description perfectly had recently been stolen from a neighboring region. It seemed certain that the escaped inmates were the culprits.

Growing more concerned by the hour, police searched a several-mile radius, looking for the truck and checking every single abandoned building they came upon in the sprawling countryside. They knew that they needed to find this girl quickly, and as the desperation grew, one officer decided to consult with a psychic detective.

It was a fine bit of irony—or perhaps fate—that the first person they called was Joyce Morgan, who just so happened to be working the case already on her own. Investigators were surprised to learn that Morgan had already gleaned quite a few details about the suspects. And when she was directed to focus on the victim, young Jennifer Barton, she was able to confirm that it was the two escaped inmates who had taken her.

Incredibly, she was able to essentially channel the girl and see through young Jennifer's eyes what she was seeing in real time. Psychic detective Morgan gave a perfect description of the inmates, then sent her mind back in time to the moment of the kidnapping. She could see Jennifer out in her yard as the suspicious green pickup truck pulled up in front of her. She perceived that Jennifer thought she knew the occupants and went over to greet them. The man in the passenger side spoke with her and persuaded her to get inside the truck. It appeared that she went willingly, of her own accord.

Whatever the circumstances of the abduction, however, it was clear that time was of the essence if Jennifer was to be recovered before things took a turn for the worse. The psychic tracked the group as they headed down the highway, looking out the window through Jennifer's eyes. She could perceive that the girl was now terrified and very much wanting the ride to end so that she could get out of the truck. Morgan had the impression that the group was on Highway 6, and she proceeded to lead detectives down that road. As they drove, she informed them that truck was now stopping at a local cemetery, and that the letters "Y-O-U" she heard repeated in her mind were somehow connected to that cemetery.

The cops were both bewildered and disturbed by this revelation, but they were open to following any lead in the kidnapping. When they eventually did come across a cemetery off the highway, they pulled in to investigate. Right in the middle of the graveyard, they were amazed to find a prominent tombstone with the name "Youtsey." The psychic detective immediately realized that this was the name from which the letters "Y-O-U" had bled through to her consciousness.

As telling as that fact was, the fugitives and their hostage were now long gone. Morgan has the distinct feeling that they were heading north by northwest, so the pursuers headed in that direction. The team was just 15 miles away when they received word that the truck had been spotted in a motel parking lot. However, the suspects themselves were nowhere to be seen.

The escapees then led the team on a cross-country chase in which they changed stolen vehicles like most people change their clothes. During the course of this chase, Morgan received the alarming impression that Jenifer had left her body and was no longer among the living. When she asked the girl to tell her where she was, she received the message that her remains were lying in an open field.

The trail led from Louisiana through Nebraska and all the way to Oklahoma, finally coming to an end when a quick-thinking policeman in Texas attempted to pull over a suspicious vehicle. This led to a high-speed chase before the occupants jumped out and fled on foot. Fugitive Roy Moore was apprehended by the officer on the scene after a short chase, but Billy Wilson was able to outmaneuver police and got away.

Unsure where the dangerous fellow might end up, authorities once again consulted Joyce Morgan for clues. This time, however, a local woman who was a good shot with a gun beat the psychic to the punch. Wilson had broken into her house during the early morning hours, and when the woman heard a disturbance she confronted him. Wilson lunged at her with a knife, but the woman had her gun already trained on his head. She shot him right between the eyes and he was dead before he hit the ground.

That was the end of the line for Wilson, and his compatriot Roy Moore was already behind bars. The only thing left to close out the case was to locate Jennifer Barton. Sadly enough, the psychic detective's vision proved correct once again. Just like the Morgan had described, Jennifer's remains were discovered in an open field.

Just before this discovery, Morgan had received the impression that Jennifer would be found at a place called "Roberts Farm," and indeed her skull was found by a farmer named Roberts on his land. It was not a happy ending for Jennifer Barton's family, but thanks to this psychic detective, Jennifer could at least be put to rest.

What Happened to Patrick?

His name was Patrick McNeil. He was a well-connected young man; his father had political ties, and his mother was deeply rooted in the Catholic Church. But when he disappeared in one of the biggest metropolitan areas in the world, New York City, he was just a living needle in a haystack—at least, everyone hoped that he was still living. But after Patrick didn't show up for work or class after a night out with friends, things were looking bleak.

Fearing the worst, his family immediately began searching for him. They even put up a $10,000 reward for his safe return. Unlike other missing persons cases that the police department might be tempted to put on the back burner, this case was given preferential treatment from the beginning due to Patrick's background. The leading theory was that a political opponent of Patrick's father had arranged for the mob to kidnap the young man and hold him hostage as some sort of leverage against the senior McNeil.

Trying to avoid a crisis in city politics, the NYPD dispatched investigators to the bar where Patrick was last seen with orders to interview everyone who'd been around the young man that night. These eyewitnesses revealed that Patrick had planned on taking the train back home. At some point he had gotten into a conversation with a woman who said she wanted to ride back with him as well.

This woman became of immediate interest to the police, but when she was tracked down and questioned it was discovered that she'd never gotten on the train with Patrick after all. She said that she had excused herself to go to the bathroom just after they had agreed to travel together, and when she returned Patrick was simply gone. She didn't know if he had just stumbled off and wandered away somewhere, or if he had met some other people and left with them.

Whatever the case, she had been left high and dry—and Patrick was still nowhere to be seen. While digesting this new piece of the puzzle, detectives turned to the security cameras for which New York is famous. A frame-by-frame examination of the cameras mounted outside the bar gave them their first images of Patrick. The footage showed an obviously drunken Patrick stumbling onto the street and attempting to flag down a cab. The cab rolled up, but then appeared to refuse to give him a ride; presumably the cabbie decided he didn't want to deal with someone so drunk. At any rate, the taxi driver rolled up his window and took off, leaving the heavily inebriated Patrick to fend for himself. The police could not find any further footage of Patrick, so after he stepped out of the frame of this particular security camera he essentially disappeared.

It was then that psychic detective Mary Rose was brought forth to shed some light on the darkness of this mysterious drunken excursion. (Since Patrick was such a high-profile disappearance, the cops were unusually willing to resort to psychic assistance to pinpoint his location.) As was her procedure, Rose began by casting an astrological chart from which she would attempt to locate her target and glean information about him. The timeline she created started with his disappearance at around two in the morning on February 16th.

This enabled her to channel him and feel what he felt. She saw him walking out of the bar and attempting to hail a cab, and she got the impression that the cabbie didn't want to pick him up. Patrick then started walking aimlessly. He never got on the train, either; he just kept right on walking.

Rose went on to inform police that Patrick had not left the city—and that she had a fairly good idea of just where he might be. She kept envisioning the numbers 6 and 9, and she felt that these were very important in regard to Patrick's whereabouts. She also said that instead of heading north toward Port Chester, where he was from, he was heading south near Brooklyn. Interesting as this was, though, it didn't provide any immediately actionable information.

Meanwhile, police were vigorously checking all of the hospitals and morgues to make sure Patrick hadn't turned up at one of these facilities. They also fielded numerous calls from people who thought they'd seen the missing man, but these all turned out to be false reports. With no sign of Patrick anywhere to be found, the kidnapping theory was looking stronger and stronger.

When Patrick had been missing for five weeks and they still had no solid leads, police turned once again to psychic detective Mary Rose to see if she had received any further visions. She told them that she pictured Patrick to be near a river, probably in the vicinity of a pier of some sort. She also insisted that she kept seeing 6 and 9, and she put these elements together as the 69th Street Pier. She believed that Patrick was in real danger and needed to be found immediately.

It was now February, and the water was freezing cold. That made it all the worse when Rose refined her focus and discovered that Patrick was not only *near* the water—he was *in* the water! She felt that Patrick was cold, he was shivering, and he couldn't breathe. And as she gathered her thoughts, she now knew exactly where he would be found. He would be discovered in the East River off the 69th Street Pier, and his body would be completely lifeless.

Understandably, detectives did not pass Rose's belief that Patrick was floating dead in the river along to his family. They continued the search as if he were still alive. But three weeks later, the Army Corp of Engineers made a tragic discovery.

Piloting a schooner through the junk and debris of the East River, Captain Liz Finn noticed what looked like a dead body floating downstream. She immediately called to report the sighting, and police swarmed to the scene. Unfortunately for Patrick's family, the body was indeed his. It turned out that there had been no kidnapping after all. Patrick, in his highly intoxicated state, had simply been trying to relieve himself into the river and had accidentally fallen in and drowned in the icy water. This tragic and senseless end to a bright young life was clearly revealed by a psychic detective.

Daryl Cozart's Fickle Friends

Daryl Cozart was a devoted family man and a hard-working chef at a busy restaurant in Sharpsville, Pennsylvania. His life revolved around going to work, coming home, and spending time with his family in that same predictable order. But on March 1,

1997, Daryl did not come home after his shift, and his wife, Jeanette, immediately knew that something was terribly wrong.

She reported his disappearance to police, but they didn't seem to take it seriously. They ventured that perhaps Daryl was just out on a late-night drinking binge with his colleagues and would turn up eventually. Jeanette knew better; she knew that not returning home and not contacting his family was just not something that Daryl would do. But the police were aggravatingly adamant in their inaction, insisting that they couldn't officially classify Daryl as a missing person until he'd been gone for 72 hours.

Frustrated and wanting to take matters into her own hands, Jeanette made up flyers with her husband's name and face on the front, seeking information from anyone who might have seen Daryl. Her mother, Mary, took some of these freshly printed flyers to a local newsstand that just happened to be owned by a psychic named Mary Ellen Rodriguez. (To eliminate confusion, henceforth we'll refer to Daryl's mother-in-law as "Mary" and the psychic detective as "Rodriguez.")

Daryl had now not been heard from for two days, and Mary was just as desperate as her daughter to find some answers. She explained the situation to Rodriguez, who seemed understanding from the beginning. But when the psychic picked up the flyer to take a better look, she got a little more than even she had bargained for. Upon touching the flyer, she immediately felt a tremendous energy—and upon looking at Daryl's photo, she saw a portal of some sort open up right behind his mother-in-law!

Through this doorway she saw Daryl Cozart himself. He seemed agitated and confused, and he kept feeling around in the air as if he were searching for a door in the darkness—as if he were desperately trying to come back, to step through from the world of the dead to the land of the living. The shocked psychic could see all of this clearly, but Mary, even after turning around, had no idea what had provoked such a reaction in Rodriguez.

But for this psychic detective the bizarre show continued, and now that Daryl knew that she could see him, he began to plead with her to let his family know what had happened to him. Rodriguez obliged by telling Mary that her son-in-law was in fact dead.

When Mary got back to her distraught daughter, she was at first hesitant to burden her with such an unusual tale, but eventually told her what had occurred at the newsstand. Not knowing what to make of the story, Jeanette went to the newsstand herself to investigate first hand. As soon as Rodriguez caught sight of Jeannette, she broke down in tears, gave her a hug, and told her mournfully, "I'm sorry... I'm so sorry." Ms. Rodriguez would later explain that it was not her talking; it was Daryl speaking through her! She claims that Daryl was forcing her to channel him because he wished to express to his wife how sorry he was that he wasn't able to come back to her.

According to Rodriguez, it was hard for Daryl to accept the fact that he was dead. He was still trying to come back, but he was slowly coming to understand that he couldn't. This is a heart-wrenching scene even to contemplate, let alone to experience. As the spirit of her recently slain husband spoke to her through a psychic medium, Jeanette was obviously beside herself with emotion.

She didn't want to believe what Rodriguez was telling her, since she was still hoping against hope that her husband was still alive. Yet at the same time, she felt compelled to believe that what this psychic told her was true. Daryl sensed how torn his wife was, and in order to convince her of the truth of the situation, he supplied psychic detective Rodriguez with a clue that only Jeanette and him would know.

He suddenly began instructing Rodriguez to "Ask her about ghost—ask her about ghost!" The psychic herself did not understand the meaning of this personal bit of information, and it actually seemed pretty darn bizarre that a ghost was instructing her to ask his widowed wife "about ghost."

But as soon as she said, "He is wanting me to ask you about 'ghost'? Is there any significance to anything called 'ghost'?" it struck an immediate nerve and Jeanette broke down in tears. It seems that the 1990 film *Ghost* was a personal favorite of the couple. The film is a romantic drama about a husband who is murdered and comes back to his wife as a ghost. The irony might seem a bit thick, but only Daryl would know about their favorite movie, and the revelation of this information coming through the conduit of the psychic detective hit Jeanette like a ton of bricks. Although Mary had come to the newsstand to pass out flyers searching for a living man, her daughter left knowing that her husband was dead.

The next day Mary Ellen Rodriguez got another visitor. This time it was the lead detective on the case, Jerry Smith. The psychic detective readily told Smith what she knew and informed him that Daryl was already dead. She also stated that she had had a vision in which Daryl was lying out in a marshy field with a gunshot wound and a rope around his neck. Wondering what secret source of information Rodriguez might have, the detective asked her point blank, "How do you know that he is dead?"

Rodriguez had a very simple answer for him: "Because he's standing right there!" She then explained how she had always been able to see apparitions and experience premonitions that most people never noticed. She had been receiving heavy doses of both ever since she had been made aware of Daryl's disappearance. Detective Smith was rather intrigued, but as he put it at the time, "You can't use apparitions or visions as testimony in a court of law."

Until he had more solid evidence that a crime had been committed, he still had to classify Daryl as simply a missing person. But while the authorities dithered, Daryl Cozart was getting restless. He began begging Rodriguez to let them know that he was dead and to keep after them until they found his body.

Knowing that the police wouldn't act until they had some evidence that Daryl had met with foul play, Rodriguez took matters into her own hands and started to search for the missing man on her own. In her free time she drove around remote regions nearby, not sure what she was looking for but feeling drawn to search nonetheless. During these investigations she would often feel a presence in the car with her that was undeniably Daryl's.

She felt that he was trying to guide her to his corpse. It must have been hard for Daryl to give directions from the other side, however. After hours of driving around in circles, Rodriguez didn't seem any closer to finding him than the police were. She felt Daryl growing more and more frustrated. It was like the solution was on the tip of his tongue but he couldn't quite get it out.

One day she felt his presence in the car with her much stronger than usual, and then Daryl inexplicably began to scream, "It's fickle! It's fickle!" The startled psychic detective didn't know what to make of this statement. Perhaps the spirit was remarking upon the fickleness of the search effort being waged on his behalf?

The ghost did not elaborate, however, and the search continued to go nowhere.

Police were making little progress in their own investigation. After questioning everyone that Daryl had worked with, they concluded that he didn't have any enemies. He seemed to be a universally well-liked guy, and no one appeared to have any motive whatsoever to do him any harm. But they did discover one important fact: the last person to have seen Daryl alive was a waitress at his restaurant named Cynthia. She claimed that Daryl had offered to give her a ride home, she agreed, he dropped her off, and that was the last time she'd seen him.

But Daryl's ghost was already telling a different story. Through further visions and visitations, he informed psychic detective Mary Ellen Rodriguez that he had met a rather grisly fate. He had been shot and hung.

After leaving these impressions, Daryl seemed to grow more agitated and impatient with the investigation. He began to manifest himself by banging on the walls of the psychic's home and periodically ringing her phone. He apparently wanted to make it perfectly clear that his soul would not be able to rest until his body was found. Not knowing what else to do, Rodriguez renewed her own personal search.

As she scoured the area one day, she suddenly felt like Daryl was trying to let her know that she was close. She heard him tell her, "It's right around here—this is where they left me." A few days later, though, she still hasn't located Daryl's body. Getting frustrated, she asked Daryl to give her more easily recognizable clues. And then, as if in response, she came across a shoe in the middle of a field. The shoe was very conspicuous, and she noticed that its toe pointed toward the west. Just as she was taking this in, she heard Daryl's voice advising her, "Go west."

Shortly thereafter, police found Daryl's van in the same area that Rodriguez had been directed to. They discovered blood on the doors, which they realized was important because it indicated an unusual sort of struggle. They were finally certain that Daryl Cozart had met with foul play. With his bloody vehicle found, all that remained was the discovery of Daryl's body.

And Daryl was still making it clear to psychic detective Marry Ellen Rodriguez that he wouldn't rest until that had been accomplished. She was driving to church on the following Sunday when Daryl's ghost began filing her mind with images of high grass and a little fence off the side of a road somewhere. She heard Daryl telling her that this was where his body was located. As she continued on her way to church, she felt as if he was grabbing the steering wheel and forcing her to turn around. He told her to go to the police department and tell them to search the location he'd indicated. This psychic detective was a woman of faith, however, and she wasn't going to be deterred from her church service!

So it was that she supposedly struck a deal with the ghost, telling him that she would go right after the service. Daryl responded that his wife had bought a new pinstripe suit for him, and he wanted to wear it at his funeral. The psychic had the morbid impression that Daryl feared his body would be too badly decomposed for an open-casket funeral if it wasn't found soon. This fact seemed to bother him more than anything else.

The very next day, through the providence of a passing truck driver, the mystery of where Daryl's body was located was finally put to rest. Passing by a forlorn stretch of road near the Ohio/Pennsylvania border, the trucker found Daryl lying in the brush much like Rodriguez had envisioned.

Even though this find did bring some sense of closure for Daryl's family, it also allowed the final reality of his death to set in. They were beyond themselves with grief and despair. And the condition that this husband and father was found in certainly did not help matters. Just as Rodriguez had predicted, he had been shot in the head as well as having a rope tied around his neck.

This was not exactly Sunday best material, but Daryl was simply happy to be found with his body still intact enough to have an open casket at his funeral. It might seem strange that a ghost would even worry about such things, but who knows? Maybe the sense of closure that a traditional funeral service provides really is a crucial aspect of passing over to the other side. Perhaps this is why slain spirits haunt the Earth until their hidden remains are uncovered.

But the funeral wasn't the end of the story. On the day that Daryl's body was discovered, Rodriguez was besieged with a series of visions that showed her exactly how he had died. She saw him walking into a trap, being set up. He went into a home and was led to a basement, where he was shot several times by people that he had trusted. She heard the phrase "Fickle! Fickle! It's fickle!" ring in her mind once again. Was Daryl referring to the fickleness of his former friends who had led him to the slaughter?

It turned out that one of these so-called friends—or at least a friend of a friend—was already communicating with police. After hearing the news that Daryl's body had been discovered, he was so overcome with guilt that he felt he had to come forward. This man had not been involved in the actual murder; he had been recruited to move the body. According to this witness, a friend of his had asked him to come over to move some furniture. The man reported that this "friend" had him go down to the garage and clean out a van. The van was Daryl's, and inside this van was a large tarp rolled up like a piece of carpet.

The friend directed the witness to help him move this rolled up tarp out of the van. When he picked up his end of the bundle, he was shocked to feel what he believed to be legs wrapped up inside. He was forced to ask the incredible question, "Is this a person?" Amazingly enough, after his friend admitted that there was indeed a body wrapped in the tarp he was moving, the witness didn't ask any more questions; he simply proceeded to help with the disposal of the dead body.

The friend's name was Frank Fickle, and as soon as the psychic detective was informed of this development it suddenly all made sense to her. Daryl wasn't repeating "It's fickle" as some sort of post-mortem commentary on the fickleness of life, love and relationships; he was trying to tell her that his killer was a man named Fickle! She had never imagined that "fickle" would be someone's name.

Of course, the skeptic might ask: If the deceased Daryl truly was communicating with her then why didn't he just come right out and say "I was murdered by a man named Frank Fickle" instead of being so vague? In defense of psychic detectives, it seems to take a tremendous amount of energy for the deceased to communicate through the barrier that separates life from death. Much of the information is filtered and sanitized as a result, usually leaving only the vaguest of impressions.

This is also the reason why most of us wouldn't perceive any communication whatsoever from a ghost screaming at us from beyond. The fact that even the best of clairvoyants only receive bits and pieces indicates that it takes quite a bit of talent just to hear anything at all! So in that sense, Rodriguez was lucky to get "It's fickle!" when most of us would have gotten absolutely nothing.

As soon as detectives assigned to Daryl's case learned of Frank Fickle's existence, they sent a team of forensics experts to comb through his house. Although the home had recently—and suspiciously—been deep cleaned, they managed to detect faint traces of blood spatter in the basement. As grisly as it sounds, a piece of scalp was also recovered, found stuck up in the rafters, as if the small piece of flesh had been turned into a projectile by the force of a bullet entering someone's skull. Perhaps even more telling, they recovered a men's bandanna with a bullet hole in it. It was then verified that this bandanna had belonged to Daryl.

After accumulating this damning evidence, police arranged an interview with Frank Fickle's wife—who was none other than Cynthia the waitress. This time they managed to get the truth out of her. She hadn't just been dropped off by Daryl; she had also invited him into her home to smoke some marijuana. In an apparent setup, she had Daryl wait in the basement while she got her husband. Frank walked down the basement stairs and immediately opened fire on Daryl. As a macabre afterthought, he then put a rope around Daryl's neck and hung him from the rafters, where he proceeded to use his corpse for target practice.

Fickle was arrested on March 12, 1997. He was subsequently tried and convicted of Daryl's murder and sentenced to life in prison. Daryl had received justice—and his body had been recovered just in time to wear his favorite pinstripe suit at his funeral. In the end, this bit of finality may have been all that his spirit wanted. His friends may have been Fickle, but through the help of a psychic detective, at least Daryl was able to see closure before it was too late.

Just a Case of Extrasensory Perception

Although history is full of seers, prophets, and visionaries who claimed to be able to perceive things from beyond, the term extrasensory perception was first used in a scientific sense by British paranormal researcher Sir Richard Burton in 1879. In 1892, the term was adopted by a French researcher to describe subjects who had been hypnotized and put into a sleep like state, yet were somehow still able to perceive things far outside the normal purview of the physical senses.

When it comes to just who has ESP and who can use it, however, there are two schools of thought. Some theorize that everyone is psychic, but there are just as many others who claim that ESP is a result of some unknown genetic trait that runs in families: You are either born with it or you are not. Many of the psychic detectives presented in this book are of the latter belief. Indeed, many have mothers, fathers or other relatives who had just as much intuitive power as they themselves, which does seem to indicate that the ability was somehow passed down.

This concept was elaborated on in depth in famed geneticist Dean Hamer's tour de force *The God Gene: How Faith is Hardwired into our Genes*. In this book, Hamer presents us with the idea that a bent toward the spiritual and the mystical depends on a specific gene called vesicular monoamine transporter 2, commonly known as VMAT2. According to Hamer and his fellow researchers, this gene is activated by slight alterations in monoamine levels. Incredibly, these scientists have proposed that the more monoamine that you have focused on your VMAT2 gene, the stronger your connection to God, the spiritual, the Universe—whatever you want to call it.

But as the stories in this book have proven, whatever it is that these psychic detectives are tapping in to, it brings them some incredible results. When families are suffering because their loved ones have gone missing or been murdered, it doesn't really matter how you classify it. You can call it extrasensory perception, you can call it the God gene, but they call it getting back their much-needed peace of mind and being able to sleep at night.

Thank you for reading!

Also by Jack Smith

Just click on the book cover to check any of them out.

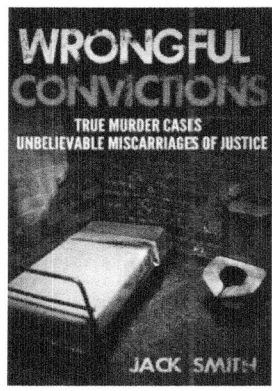

Appendix A: Further Reading and Resources

In this final section of the book, I would like to pass along some of the reading material and other resources that allowed me to write it. If the subject of psychic detectives is one that holds great interest for you, you owe it to yourself to read the following selections as well.

***Psychic Detectives: The Mysterious Use of Paranormal Phenomena in Solving True Crimes.* Jenny Randles and Peter Hough**
This book presents a thorough and truly fascinating take on the psychic detective. It takes us from the days of Sherlock Holmes—when paranormal research first came into vogue—to the information age of the present, when doors have opened for clairvoyant crime fighters like never before. I have gleaned an incredible amount of information from this veritable encyclopedia of the psychic detective, and if you are interested in the subject it is a highly recommended read.

***The God Gene: How Faith is Hardwired into our Genes.* Dean Hamer**
In this book Hamer presents a stunning hypothesis. He believes that he has located a gene that not only facilitates belief in the paranormal, but perhaps establishes a connection to it! According to Hamer, we all have a specific gene that responds to the spiritual and the mystical; that essentially allows us to connect to God, or in its simplest terms "a universal source of knowledge greater than ourselves." Psychic detectives often describe their ability as tapping into some great cosmic store of knowledge, as if they are downloading the information from some universal mainframe. Could Hamer have discovered the

actual gene that allows psychic detectives to do this? It's a fascinating read not to be missed!

ESPD Blue. **Stephan Schwartz**
In this short but informative narrative, Schwartz highlights the powerful ways in which intuitive individuals and psychics are being used by police forces. Most fascinating of all, Schwartz even proposes that *all* police undergo some form of psychic training, creating a true ESPD Blue! Some fascinating concepts are presented here!

Printed in Great Britain
by Amazon